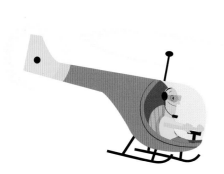

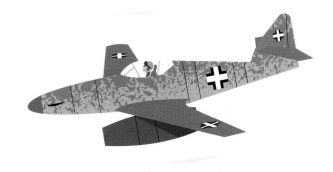

A Journey Through
TRANSPORT

by Chris Oxlade
Illustrated by John Haslam

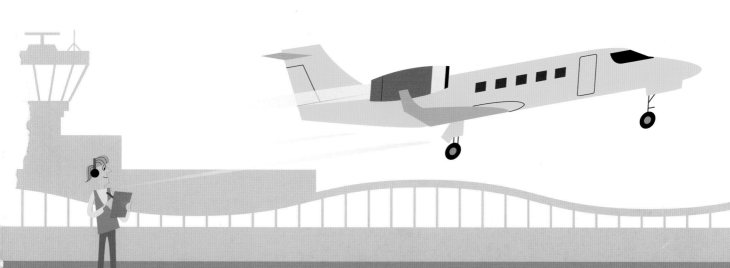

Quarto is the authority on a wide range of topics.

Quarto educates, entertains and enriches the lives of
our readers—enthusiasts and lovers of hands-on living.

www.quartoknows.com

First published in the UK in 2017 by QED Publishing

A catalogue record for this book is available from the British Library.

ISBN 978 1 78493 812 3

Publisher: Maxime Boucknooghe
Editorial Director: Laura Knowles
Art Director: Susi Martin
Editor: Carly Madden
Consultant: Oliver Green

Originated in Hong Kong by Bright Arts.
Printed and bound in China by Toppan Leefung Printing Ltd.
10 9 8 7 6 5 4 3 2 1   17 18 19 20 21

Contents

All aboard!

Jump on! We're ready to set off on a journey through the world of transport. Let's discover the amazing cars, trains, planes and ships that carry us on land, through the air and across the sea.

Journey Through Space

As well as seeing shiny new transport, we will travel back in time and see the weird and wonderful machines from the past.

Walking and riding

Many thousands of years
ago there were no cars or
buses, or planes, or ships.
Nothing! People simply
walked when they went
hunting for animals
or gathering fruits
and seeds.

People learned to train
wild animals to help them.
Horses, mules, camels,
yaks and llamas trudged
along with heavy loads on
their backs. Animals are
still used to carry goods in
many parts of the world.

Giddy up! People also
learned how to ride on animals
such as horses and camels.
Then they could travel all day
without getting tired.

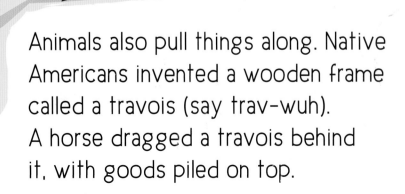

Animals also pull things along. Native
Americans invented a wooden frame
called a travois (say trav-wuh).
A horse dragged a travois behind
it, with goods piled on top.

Rolling wheels

People began to make simple wheels about 5,500 years ago. The wheels were made of solid wood, or planks joined together. People built simple carts with the wheels, and piled them high with luggage to carry.

Brave Greek and Roman warriors rode into battle in speedy chariots. The chariots had wheels with spokes, like modern bicycle wheels.

Stand aside! Here comes a stagecoach!

In the 1600s, stagecoaches sped along the roads, pulled by teams of galloping horses. The roads were rough and muddy, and passengers had a very bumpy ride.

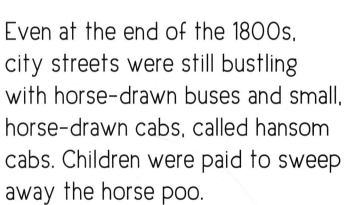

Even at the end of the 1800s, city streets were still bustling with horse-drawn buses and small, horse-drawn cabs, called hansom cabs. Children were paid to sweep away the horse poo.

Yuck!

The first motor cars

A carriage without a horse? That's exactly what the first cars were! A German inventor called Karl Benz built the first-ever car in 1886. He called the car the Benz Motorwagen.

What's that noise?

To begin with, the loud 'putt-putt' sound of car engines took horses and people by surprise.

In Britain, a person had to walk in front of a car, holding up a red flag to warn people that it was coming!

Early cars were expensive. Only rich people could afford to buy them. An American carmaker called Henry Ford changed all that. In 1908 he started making a small, cheap car called the Model T.

In Britain, Charles Rolls and Henry Royce decided to build a big, comfy car. They called their beautiful machine the Rolls-Royce Silver Ghost.

Cars, big and small

Beep, beep! The roads today are busy with cars of all shapes and sizes. Most cars have an engine at the front, powered by fuel. The engine turns the front wheels to make the car go.

Cars with petrol or diesel engines give out dirty, smelly gases that are bad for our environment and health. Electric cars give out no harmful gases.

They are much cleaner but you have to keep recharging their batteries to power the motor.

Sleek sports cars are built for speed. Some sports cars are convertible, too. The driver can fold the roof down in warm weather to enjoy the sunshine.

Four-by-four cars have big wheels and chunky tyres for driving along rough tracks, through mud and across fields. They're great for farmers!

13

Large lorries and busy buses

Lorries are big, tough machines! They carry parcels, food, cars, rubble and all sorts of other things. An articulated lorry has a tractor cab, where the driver sits. Behind is a trailer for cargo.

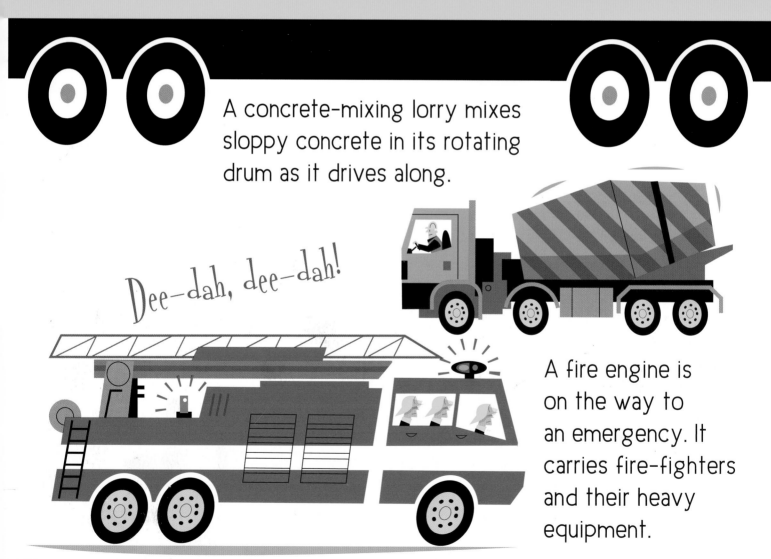

A concrete-mixing lorry mixes sloppy concrete in its rotating drum as it drives along.

Dee-dah, dee-dah!

A fire engine is on the way to an emergency. It carries fire-fighters and their heavy equipment.

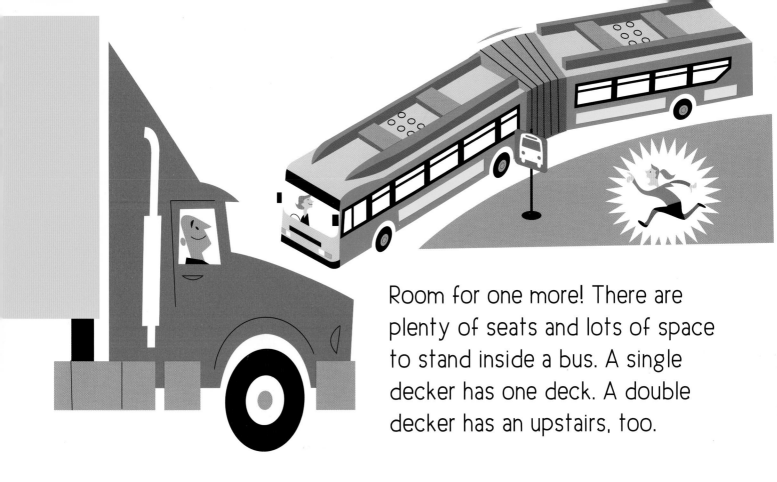

Room for one more! There are plenty of seats and lots of space to stand inside a bus. A single decker has one deck. A double decker has an upstairs, too.

Coaches carry passengers on long journeys. They have comfy seats and a toilet on board, television screens and wi-fi. Sit back and enjoy the ride…

Pedalling along

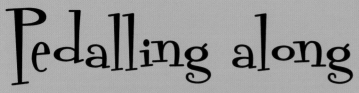

That's odd! The first bicycles didn't have any pedals. The rider pushed on the ground with their feet to get going. These bicycles were called hobbyhorses. They were invented about 200 years ago.

Climbing on and off the seat of a penny-farthing bicycle was a bit tricky! This bicycle was named after two coins, a penny, which was big, and a farthing, which was small. Can you guess why?

In the 1880s, a bicycle was invented that was very like the bicycles we ride today. It had pedals, and a chain, and brakes for stopping.

A tandem is a bicycle for two riders.

Today, road bicycles are light and have thin tyres, which allows them to zoom along fast! Multi-terrain bikes have tough frames and chunky tyres, so they can tackle bumps and jumps.

Motorcycles and more

The very first motorcycles looked like bicycles, but with an engine joined on to make them go.

Motorcycles got bigger and bigger, and faster and faster. The Indian Chief was a monster motorcycle of the 1940s. It sped past with a deep, noisy growl from its engine!

A modern sports motorcycle is super-fast.

Swish!

A snowmobile skims across the snow. It's like a motorcycle for the winter! It has skis at the front and spinning tracks at the back that push it along.

A quad bike is a motorcycle with four wheels instead of two wheels. Farmers love quad bikes. They are great for zipping through mud and up and down steep hills.

Steam trains

The first trains began steaming along around 200 years ago. Chuff, chuff! The passengers often sat on hard wooden benches in wagons, with steam and smoke swirling around them.

Giant locomotives called Big Boys pulled trains in the 1940s in the USA. They were the longest steam locomotives ever built!

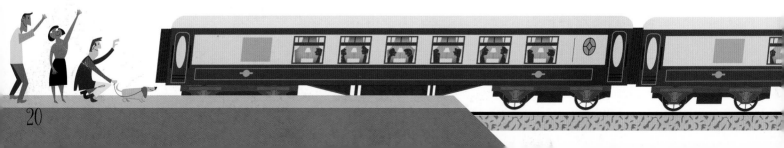

In a steam locomotive, a roaring fire boils water to make hot steam. The steam pushes pistons in and out of cylinders. The pistons turn the locomotive's wheels.

Firebox Boiler Cylinder

Piston

Wheels

All aboard the Orient Express! This famous train steamed from Paris in France to Istanbul in Turkey. Passengers slept in luxurious cabins and enjoyed yummy food in the restaurant car.

Modern trains

Gone in a flash! Express trains are super-fast passenger trains that zip between towns and cities. The electricity for their motors comes from cables above the track.

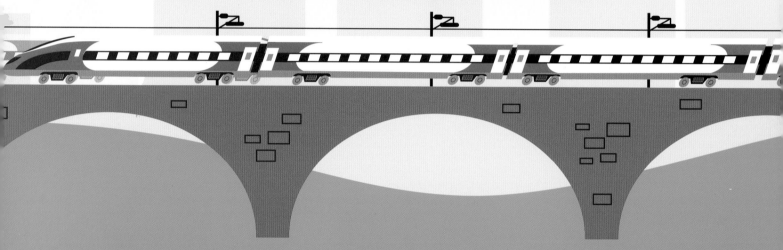

A freight train is made up of lots of wagons full of coal, or gravel, or grain.

A locomotive with a huge, powerfu diesel engine pulls the train along.

Some trains rattle along in tunnels below city streets. They stop to pick up passengers at stations deep under ground. When it's busy the passengers are squashed into the carriages!

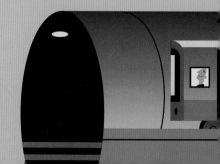

Many trains have diesel-electric engines.

Maglev trains have no wheels! Instead, they float above the track using the power of magnets. They zoom along faster than most other express trains.

The biggest freight trains are more than a kilometre long.

Early boats

Ahoy there! Thousands of years ago people made rafts out of logs or bundles of reeds. They also hollowed out tree trunks to make dug-out canoes.

Sails were invented more than 5,000 years ago.

The first sailing ships had just one square sail. The crew had to row with oars when the wind stopped blowing. It would have been very hard work.

Around 500 years ago, brave explorers sailed out into the stormy oceans. They sailed in small sailing ships called caravels and carracks.

Beautiful clipper ships were the fastest sailing ships. They had lots of sails to catch the wind. They carried tea and wool between Europe, America and Asia.

Steamships

Time for a paddle! The first steamships had paddle wheels on each side to push them along. They were built about 200 years ago.

Most steamships also carried sails because their steam engines sometimes broke down.

In America, paddle steamers called packet boats chugged along rivers such as the Mississippi.

They carried passengers and cargo. Some had a huge paddle wheel on the back.

The steamship *Great Eastern* was launched in 1858. It was a giant. There was space on board for an amazing 4,000 passengers. *Great Eastern* made other ships look tiny.

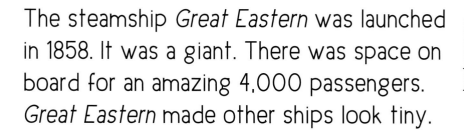

In the 1930s, huge steam-powered liners criss-crossed the Atlantic Ocean between Europe and the USA. The liners were luxurious and beautiful, like hotels at sea.

Modern ships and boats

Today all sorts of ships and boats sail on the world's oceans, lakes and rivers. Let's take a look at some of them.

Sailing yachts, powerboats and rowing boats carry just a few people. Sailing boats are pushed along by their sails, which catch the wind. Powerboats use engines. Rowing boats are powered by people – muscle power!

Cruise ships are like giant floating hotels with restaurants, swimming pools, gyms and shops. The biggest cruise ships are longer than three football pitches.

Cargo ships carry all sorts of goods around the world.

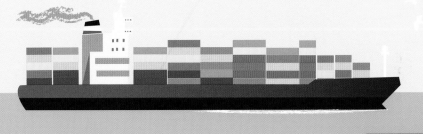

Ferries carry people and vehicles across rivers and seas. Most ferries have doors in the front and back that open to let vehicles drive on and off.

Ducking under

Going down! Submarines and submersibles are boats that dive under the water.

An American inventor called David Bushnell built a simple wooden submarine called *Turtle* in 1775. Only one person could squeeze inside.

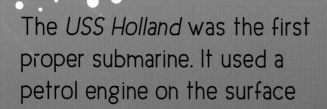

The *USS Holland* was the first proper submarine. It used a petrol engine on the surface and an electric motor under the water. Six crewmembers worked inside the hot, smelly submarine.

A modern submarine can stay underwater for months without coming to the surface. It has hydroplanes like a fish's fins. They help it to dive down or rise towards the surface.

In 2012 a submersible called Deepsea Challenger dived 11 kilometres down into the ocean!

A submersible is a small submarine for exploring the gloomy ocean depths. Some submersibles have space for a crew. Other submersibles are robot vehicles, or they are remote-controlled.

Hot-air balloons and airships

The French Montgolfier brothers built the first hot-air balloon that carried a person into the air. It was made of paper! It first took off in 1783.

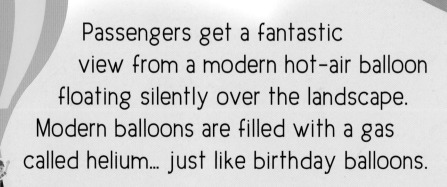

Passengers get a fantastic view from a modern hot-air balloon floating silently over the landscape. Modern balloons are filled with a gas called helium… just like birthday balloons.

An airship floats in the air like a hot-air balloon. But it also has an engine that pushes it along. Frenchman Henri Giffard built a wonderful steam-powered airship in 1852. He flew it over Paris.

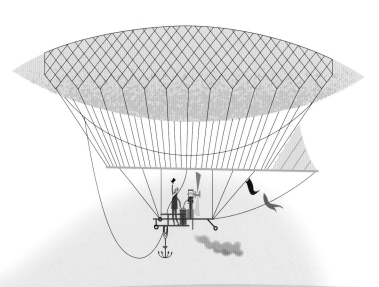

In the 1930s, giant airships carried passengers on exciting journeys across the oceans. The *Hindenburg* airship, built in Germany, was the biggest flying airship ever! Inside were cabins, a dining room and a luxury lounge.

The first planes

Ready for take-off! An aeroplane is a flying machine with wings that keep it in the air.

The first aeroplanes were gliders. A glider doesn't have an engine. It glides through the air like a giant paper plane!

Two American brothers called Orville and Wilbur Wright built a famous aeroplane, called *Flyer*. It made its first flight in 1903. It only stayed in the air for 12 seconds, but it was the first proper aeroplane flight.

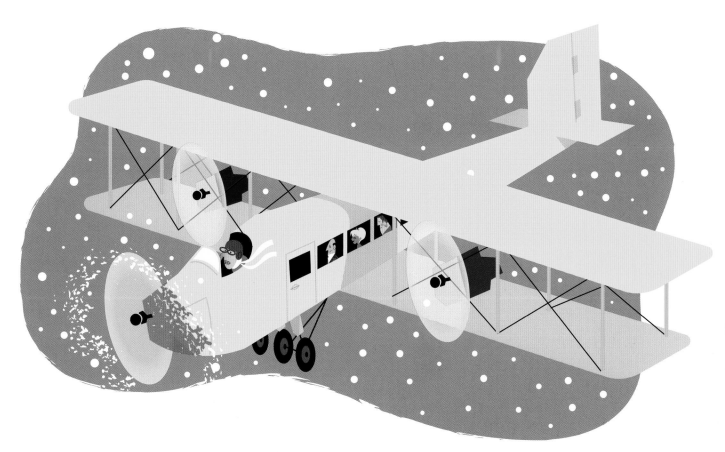

In the 1920s, airliners started carrying passengers between towns and cities. On some airliners the poor pilot had to sit outside, even in winter. Brrr!

This is a small modern aeroplane. Its wings lift it into the air, while the engine pulls it along. Its tailplane and fin keep it flying in a straight line.

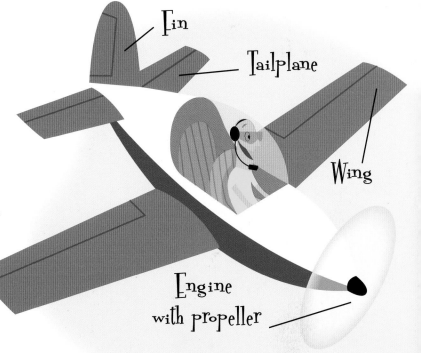

Fin

Tailplane

Wing

Engine with propeller

Fast jets, jumbo jets

The incredible jet engine was invented in the 1930s. Soon many aeroplanes had jet engines instead of propellers.

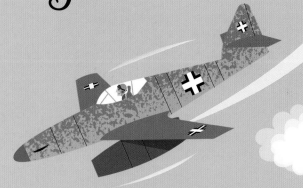

The first jet planes fought in World War II.

A roaring jet engine sucks in air at the front and blasts a jet of gas out of the back with a loud rumble. This pushes the aircraft forwards.

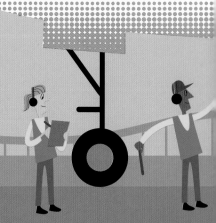

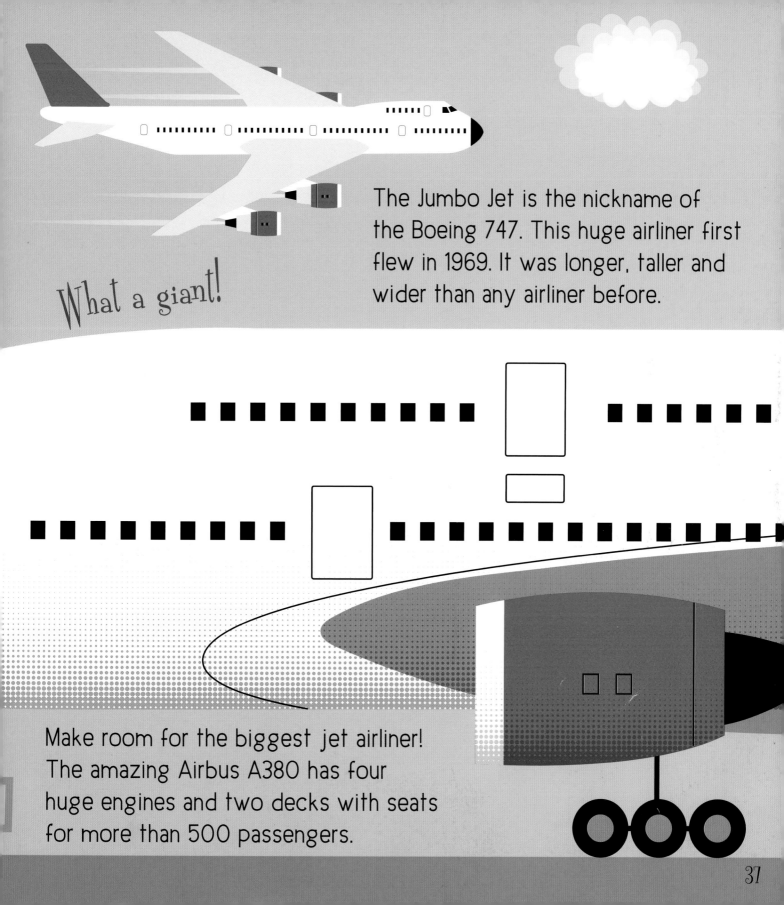

The Jumbo Jet is the nickname of the Boeing 747. This huge airliner first flew in 1969. It was longer, taller and wider than any airliner before.

What a giant!

Make room for the biggest jet airliner! The amazing Airbus A380 has four huge engines and two decks with seats for more than 500 passengers.

Whirling helicopters

A helicopter is lifted into the air by whirling rotor blades. The first helicopter was built by a French bicycle maker, Paul Cornu. His invention looked very wobbly and dangerous! Modern helicopters are more solid!

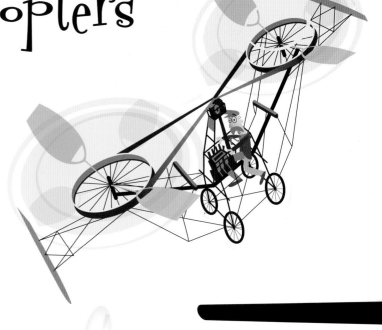

Rescue helicopters and air ambulances can help people in trouble at sea, or in the wilderness. Rescuers are lowered down from the helicopter to pluck up people and carry them to safety.

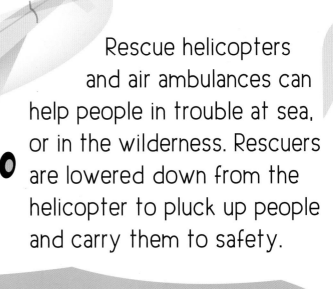

Chop, chop, chop! Here comes help!

Armies have giant helicopters for moving heavy equipment around the battlefield. This helicopter is a Chinook. It has two main rotors and space inside for soldiers and their kit. Chinooks are very noisy!

Blasting into space

We've seen lots of amazing vehicles that transport us on land, on water and in the air. Now hold tight... it's time to grab a spacecraft and blast off into space!

Russian cosmonaut Yuri Gagarin was the first human to go to space. He travelled in a Vostok spacecraft, in 1961.

Three American astronauts, Neil Armstrong, Buzz Aldrin and Michael Collins, sped to the Moon and back in their Apollo spacecraft. Armstrong and Aldrin landed on the Moon's dusty surface.

Space shuttles flew into space between 1981 and 2012. A space shuttle took off like a rocket, but landed back on Earth gently, like a glider.

Astronauts live on the International Space Station. The Space Station whizzes round the Earth fifteen times every day!

Spacecraft carry astronauts to the Space Station and back to Earth.

Future transport

Can you imagine what cars, trains, ships and planes will be like in the future?

In the sky we might see lots of robot aeroplanes and helicopters, called drones. They will be delivering parcels to homes and offices.

On the roads we may see cars zooming along with nobody in control. These driverless cars will have a computer that controls them.

One day you might holiday in space! Perhaps you could take a sightseeing tour to see an amazing view of the stars.

In the future, astronauts may set off to visit the planet Mars. The journey to Mars and back will take over a year. One day, astronauts might even set up home on Mars.

Can you spot these vehicles?

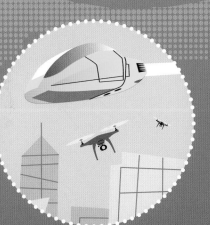

Can you work out what they are?

Quiz time!

Can you answer these questions about transport?
Here's a hint – you can find all the answers in this book.

1. What did Roman warriors ride into battle?

2. What was the name of the famous car that Henry Ford built?

3. What sort of machine was a penny farthing?

4. What was the longest steam locomotive ever built?

5. How many passengers could the *Great Eastern* carry?

6. Which submarine dived 11 kilometres deep in the ocean?

7. What was the Montgolfier brothers' balloon made from?

8. Who was the first human to go into space?

Answers

1. A chariot. 2. The Model-T.
3. A bicycle. 4. The Big Boy.
5. 4,000. 6. Deepsea Challenger.
7. Paper. 8. Yuri Gagarin.

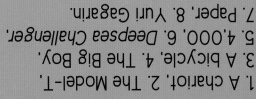